Hope in the City

A Response to the Archbishop's Commission Report on Urban Priority Areas, *Faith in the City,* **(Church House Publishing 1985)**

Edited by

Greg Forster

Convenor, Grove Ethics Group

GROVE BOOKS LIMITED
Bramcote   Nottingham   NG9 3DS

CONTENTS

ACKNOWLEDGEMENTS

Quotations from *Faith in the City* are reproduced by kind permission of the publishers, Church House Publishing, London.

THE COVER PICTURE

. . . is by Steve Pickering

First Impression April 1986

ISSN 0305–4241

ISBN 1 85174 025 2

1. INTRODUCTION
by Richard Higginson

Faith in the City has been acclaimed as a landmark in the life of the Church of England, a prophetic survey that must be acted upon urgently and decisively. It appears to have highlighted poverty, deprivation, oppression and despair in our Urban Priority Areas in a way which has enlightened and challenged many, not only Christians among them. The writers of this booklet are certainly at one in their belief that *Faith in the City* is a report of great significance. Its merits are not difficult to identify. It is painstakingly thorough and judiciously fair in its assessment of the decline and decay in our inner cities. It neither minimizes the responsibility of the church in neglecting inner city needs nor shrinks from making far-reaching criticisms of recent Government policies towards Urban Priority Areas. *Faith in the City* is a report which should be read, and read widely. We hope that it will be.

Nevertheless, for all its strengths, we question whether the Archbishop's Commission on Urban Priority Areas got all its emphases right. *Faith in the City* runs the risk of not being the spur to commitment and action which it was intended to be because of over-emphases and under-emphases in various directions. We note that a widespread initial reaction of individuals and church gatherings to the Report's impressive list of recommendations has been: how does this affect us? What can I, we, or our church, *do*? People have been left feeling rather numbed. We believe that this is because so many of the Report's recommendations are aimed at centralized authority, whether in church or state. They are calls for a redistribution of resources here, an increase in spending there, an appointment of new officer, committee, or programme, somewhere else. The cumulative effect of this top-heavy bureaucratic emphasis is to leave the ordinary man in the pew or street feeling rather helpless, or to reinforce that feeling.

We do not wish to be misunderstood here. We recognize the need for reform at a structural level and for a radical change in policies by central government. We believe that the facts and figures which have been assembled so scrupulously by the Archbishop's Commission do add up to a formal indictment of recent Government policy in many areas. The hard evidence suggests that the social consequences of conservative exaltation of individual self-interest and competition have not been benign, as was predicted, but disastrous; that particular measures in the tax, social security and public spending areas have served to widen the gulf between rich and poor in our society; and that where an effort has been made to remedy deprivation, as with the Urban Programme, this has often been offset by cuts elsewhere, e.g., in the Rate Support Grant. ACUPA has done the country a service in documenting this evidence so thoroughly while refraining from addressing the issues in narrow party political terms.

We do not doubt that a redirection of national resources could lead to the creation of more jobs, to an improvement in the public housing stock, and so on. But what Urban Priority Areas need above all is a transformation in their inhabitants' morale, a belief that *they* can do something to change their lot. And as the Report notes, encouraging things are happening in Urban Priority Areas, both on a church and a community level. The Report ends with the affirmation that the members of the Commission have found faith in the city.

Unfortunately, most of the specific references to constructive local developments are tantalizingly fleeting. The Report affirms the value of a theology of story but then tells surprisingly few stories! We realize that its writers are limited by constraints of space but if successful—however small-scale—projects in job creation, health care or community care had been documented in more detail, with an exploration of the philosophy or Christian thinking which lay behind them, the Report might have provided more of an inspiration for local initiative and action.

In the pages which follow we aim to provide not so much an alternative (and certainly not a counter-blast) to *Faith in the City*, as a supplement. Chris Sugden welcomes the way that the Report sets theology in the context of mission; he emphasizes the idea of 'good news for the poor' as a key to understanding the meaning of the Kingdom of God; but he then goes on to outline a theology which places greater emphasis on personal identity and dignity, leading to personal enabling and the exercise of stewardship, than is found in the ACUPA Report. Roy McCloughry writes of the psychological dangers which ensue when attention is focussed overwhelmingly on a *structural* cause of our problems and key to their solution. He explores the place of personal responsibility in the political and economic spheres of life, and asks what kind of changes we are really expecting in Urban Priority Areas.

Michael Paget-Wilkes questions the Report's implicit assumption that the strengths of the Church of England are mainly to be found in middle-class congregations, and that it is the inner-city congregations which have most to learn and to receive. He suggests that beneath the apparent weakness of many Urban Priority Area churches there actually lie considerable strengths, and that the depth of commitment and authentic spirituality shown by Christians there represent a major challenge to Christians in more comfortable situations. Lastly, Greg Forster provides some examples of local initiative and faith which give an indication of what can and is being done. Small businesses, resource centres for the unemployed, local churches overcoming the barriers and suspicions of race . . . such are the things which boost morale and restore self-dignity and group-dignity among people in these areas.

We offer this booklet in a positive spirit, as an exercise in creative dialogue with the Report. Our overall aim is to establish ground not only for faith, but also for *hope*, in our city.

2. THEOLOGY IN THE CONTEXT OF MISSION
by Chris Sugden

Faith in the City is welcome. The Report highlights deprivation and oppression. Disadvantaged people caught in this way have a prior claim on
Christians. For Jesus entrusts us with good news to the poor. This
booklet is offered as a positive response in creative dialogue with the
Report. It seeks to complement the Report by building on its insights. It
suggests a number of areas of the Report which require further discus-
sion. The contributors offer their reflections in the spirit of welcome to
strengthen the understanding of and commitment to mission and faith in
the city.

The contributor of this chapter on the theological rooting of the Report
writes from experience and reflection on ministry among the deprived
and oppressed in India. The list of those who submitted written evidence
to the Commission does not appear to include Christian Aid, the Church
Missionary Society, or any overseas Christian group working among the
poor and disadvantaged. This remains a weakness in the insular
approach of Christianity in these islands. This chapter offers some comments from that perspective on the Report's theology, its reading of
scripture, and its understanding of mission.

First the Report itself is most welcome because its very existence suggests that mission is the context for doing theology. It is right to say that
'abstract intellectual formulation does not necessarily have absolute
primacy in the understanding and communication of the Christian faith'
(3.37 p.65). The insight of Christians in Two-Thirds World countries is
that the context in which we are engaged in mission sets the framework
in which we come to Scripture. Thus for them the question is not 'How in
a world of reason and science can we talk of miracles', but 'what in a
situation of oppression and poverty does God require and enable us to
do?' The Report firmly impresses on us that the context of oppression in
our inner cities sets the framework for seeking to understand and obey
God's will and word. It rightly points out that the framework within which
our Church has too often worked out the faith has been the framework of
the privatized individual life (3.8 p.50). The context of faith for many
Christians in England is that Jesus brings change in our internal psychological space. In the Bible the context of faith is that God acts in the
arena of history and his action thus gives the setting for the appropriate
changes in the psychological space. By focusing on life in the inner
cities, the Report rightly insists that the life of the community we live in
sets the context for working out our theology and our practice. The
Report is right to stress that the way to do theology goes far beyond
deducing insights from scripture, fitting scripture into a kind of
systematic whole which is then applied to every circumstance.

The Willowbank Report, from an international evangelical consultation
on *Gospel and Culture,* stated,

> 'Today's readers cannot come to the text in a personal vacuum and
> should not try to. Instead they should come with an awareness of
> concerns from their cultural background, personal situation and

responsibility to others. These concerns will influence the questions which are put to the scriptures. What is received back will not be answers only, but also more questions. As we address Scripture, Scripture addresses us. We find that our culturally conditioned presuppositions are being challenged and our questions corrected. In fact, we are compelled to reformulate our previous questions and to ask fresh ones.'[1]

Some may ask 'But what has the context of inner city mission to do with us who do not live in the inner city?' Two answers may be made. One stresses that we cannot divide out city or country into hermetically sealed ghettoes. We are one nation, and Christianly we are parts of one body. The question reveals the disease of our individualism which seeks meaning for our individual lives apart from our corporate existence, or existence for our ghetto apart from the whole society. The second answer comes explicitly from a biblical viewpoint. That is that the meaning of the good news of the kingdom of God, the Gospel of the kingdom of God, is focused for everyone on what it means to poor people. In the Old Testament God's Word for the world was his action in rescuing the Hebrew slaves from Egypt.

What God was doing to bring his change to the whole world was shown by what he was doing through the people of Israel. The people of Israel were Hebrew slaves who had been rescued from Egypt. The good news to the Hebrew slaves defined the good news to everyone. In the New Testament Jesus defined his ministry as good news to the poor (Luke 4). When he replied to the messengers of John the Baptist in Luke 7.22, he gave us the authentication of his messiahship that good news was preached to the poor. (That these were the physically poor is shown by the fact that they are classified with the blind, the lame, the deaf, and the dead, which are all physical categories.)

Jesus' message to Jerusalem, the place of power, was precisely his three-year ministry among the sick and outcast of Galilee of the Gentiles. What Jesus did and taught in Galilee defined his good news for everyone. His parable of the Pharisee and the tax-collector shows this (Luke 18.9-14). For Jesus, being in the right with God was defined not by the Pharisee for the socially despised tax-collector, but by the tax-collector (in his attitude to God) for the self-righteous Pharisee. On at least two occasions Jesus identified the existence of true faith, of faith by which people should assess theirs, in Gentiles—the Syro-Phoenician woman and the Roman centurion whose servant he healed.

This good news, defined by what it means to the poor and the marginalized as the Gentiles were in Jewish society, is the good news for those who were not poor. Jesus' meeting with Zaccheus resulted in Zaccheus repaying those whom he had defrauded and sharing his goods with the poor. Jesus' good news affirmed Zaccheus' victims (who for Zaccheus had been fair game). To appropriate God's news for him, Zaccheus has to change, repay those whom he has defrauded, and share with the poor.

[1] The Willowbank Report *Gospel and Culture* (Lausanne Occasional Papers No. 2, 1978) p.11.

Paul shows the same approach in 1 Cor. 1.26, 28. 'From the human point of view, few of you were wise or powerful or of high social standing . . . God chose what the world looks down on and despises, and thinks is nothing, to destroy what the world thinks is important.' In his mission strategy, Paul specifically went to the Gentiles (whom the Jews despised) to make the Jews jealous that God's promises were being received by the Gentile dogs (Rom. 11.13-15). In Paul's letters, the meaning of justification by faith to the despised Gentiles, who could not depend on any Jewish ancestry or heritage for merit or salvation, defined the meaning of God's work in Christ for everyone (cf. Gal. 2.15ff.).

Of course the good news is addressed to everyone. No one is excluded. But it is mediated to everyone by what it means to poor people who res-pond to it. This is why Michael Paget-Wilkes' chapter on the spiritual wealth and gifts of Christians in inner city situations is so important. It is not a matter of an inverted spiritual snobbery, or a form of spiritual one-upmanship. It just is the case in the Bible that what Jesus truly means is demonstrated to everyone by what he means to poor and powerless people. That is the biblical norm. Those who are not poor or socially des-pised Christians are to take their cue from those who are. This is not the way of the world, where the powerful and successful set the values for the powerless and those perceived as failures. The picture Michael Paget-Wilkes describes is precisely the reverse of the world's way of looking at things—and we should not expect it to be otherwise.

The world's way of looking at things is to define values by the lives of the successful. But this produces a distortion in the biblical message. Bishop David Evans writes of Western formulations of the good news:

> 'In a situation of violence like that of Peru, some of the twentieth century simplifications of the Christian message are just not big enough . . .neither are they true to the fullness of the biblical gos-pel. One such simplification, the "health and wealth" gospel of some parts of the First World, has strong and blatant cultural over-tones. Another such reduces spiritual reality to "four laws" and breeds an individualistic concept of salvation which at its worst is a new form of self-centredness. Then there is the old "social gospel" which leaves out the vital ingredients of repentance, so people re-main untransformed.'[1]

The reason why the context of the inner city should set the agenda of *all* churches, is that the good news we are all to proclaim is to be shaped by what it means among poor people. This is the reason why it is sad that lessons have not been drawn in the Report from situations around the world where the gospel has deep roots among poor people.

People's Participation

One of those lessons is that a key category for interpreting and proclaim-ing the good news is the category of identity, dignity and worth. Historically speaking, in India Christian missions were the first to treat the untouchables as human beings. Lalive D'Epinay in *Haven of the Masses* (Lutterworth, 1969) notes that the reason for the phenomenal growth of Pentecostalism in Chile was that the churches gave dignity,

---

[1] 'Peru Witness for Change', in *Tranformation* Vol. 3 No. 1, p.9.

worth and a role for slum-dwellers who had been made to feel worse than rubbish. In contemporary Christian reflection on relief and development it is noted that economic projects do not of themselves enable people to develop the sense of self-worth which is crucial. Rather the development of self-worth is the foundation for every other human growth.

The Report correctly brings to our attention that lack of self-esteem is a crucial issue in the inner city and that people's participation in any effort to bring change is crucial.[1]

But unfortunately the Report does not adequately root that insight in theological or biblical themes. What is even more unfornate is that major recommendations of the Report for developing mission in the inner city focus not on people's participation but on the recruiting, training, and work of more clergy (under various titles). And the major recommendation of the report for the nation are focused in centralized bureaucratic economic programmes.[2]

Work needs to be done on biblical and theological themes of self-worth, dignity, and the life and leadership of the people of God which will promote that. This chapter will suggest some themes currently being explored.

Oppression rubs out people's dignity. Bishop Desmond Tutu points out how strip-searches of his wife and daughter under the guise of pass laws serve to trample down the identity of blacks in South Africa. In Jesus' time the term 'sinner' was used to put down people judged to be outside God's people because of some supposed ritual pollution.

The scriptures describe and interpret humanity's identity as stewards of God. In Genesis 1.26-27 humanity (men and women together) are called to be the image of God, to exercize dominion over creation, to manage creation. The term 'image' in the Ancient Near East referred to the king or the idol as the tenant of the absentee God. God's tenant, vice-regent or manager is humanity. All are called to exercise stewardship over resources. The problem is that many poor people (in our inner cities and in the Two-Thirds World) cannot exercise that stewardship. They are denied access to resources. They are denied a say in how they manage the earth. And it is no answer to this identity issue to make people consumers, receivers, dependent on hand-outs from relief agencies or the welfare state. The problem with the welfare state is that it does not go far enough to enable people to become stewards. So there is no space for them to develop a sense of fulfilment, in stewardship. One practical way this is being developed in the Two-Thirds World is through micro-loan schemes for small businesses. Of course a wider context of economic development is also needed, but the fundamental issue is that people are enabled to be stewards not receivers.

Human sin expresses itself in exercising dominion over people not resources. When Pharoah treated the Hebrew slaves as non-human resources, God's action was to give them a land and laws to enable them

---

[1] (247, (10.61 wi), 248 (10.64), 277, (12.15), 284 (12.36), 285 (12.40, 41), 286 (12.43).

[2] It is really no wonder that Government ministers thought they could 'rubbish' the Report as old-fashioned, tired, centralized policies of 40 years ago.

to be stewards. In the New Testament Paul tells us that the purpose of God is that we should be conformed to the image is his Son (Romans 8.29). Jesus is the true steward. The context of Christian discipleship is stewardship. The report stresses the importance of people's participation. Stewardship is part of the theological undergirding that it needs. The report exposes the dearth of our thinking in Christian approaches to enabling people to exercise stewardship. Both top-down management styles and centralized bureaucracy stifle this. At issue is the identity to which people are called.

The Old Testament analyzes ways in which people are robbed of their identity. Though God's purpose in giving people the land was equality, the institution of kingship with his courts and nobles began a process of centralization and impoverishment.[1] In the New Testament people were robbed of their identity by being excluded from membership of Israel as the Pharisees and scribes defined it. It was to these lost sheep, these sinners that Jesus went. And his news was that in him and through him they were welcome to God's people, God's kingdom and to be God's sons and daughters and his brothers and sisters. Those whose experience of life was that their identity was constantly rubbed out were enabled by grace to be the sons of God. Stephen Mott points out that 'in the New Testament status is the key to social ethics.'[1] Jesus' mission extended particulary to those whose status was hurt by social relationships—the sick, women, children, Samaritans. He gave them new status as Paul did to the Gentiles. 'You Gentiles are not foreigners or strangers any longer; you are now fellow-citizens with God's people and members of God's family,' (Eph. 2.19). This new status is not experienced individually. It is experienced 'in God's family'. Thus the calling of the church is to be a family where those whose identity has been rubbed out can discover a new status by grace. This is not just a romantic religious fiction. It is to be affirmed in concrete reality as Jews and Gentiles, white and black, men and women, receive from one another in one body. It is an expression of good news. It is a strategy for a church's life.

It is to be hoped that further work will be done in using this biblical resource to address British society. The report is unfortunately thin on its analysis of our society which produces oppression. It is silent on the issue of class. The church has a calling far beyond pressing government or local councils to provide community centres. It is to be that community which offers and affirms new status to those whose identity has been rubbed out by oppression. In India one of the most successful community health projects was where Christians walked outcaste women through the Gospels to show that they were the equal of anybody. By building their self-confidence and dignity the Christians gave scope for the women to teach local mothers how to combat infant mortality. Over a twenty-year period those women have been the foundation of seventeen villages turning to Christ and infant mortality being eradicated.

Similar stories could be gathered from inner-city churches in Britain. Reflections on such stories would provide a theology of story as the Report suggests.

[1] See further Klaus Nuthberger *Affluence Poverty and the Word of God* (Lutheran Publishing House 1978), *Lifestyle in the Eighties* ed. R. J. Sider (Paternoster, 1982).

[2] S. Mott, *Jesus and Social Ethics* (Grove Booklets on Ethics No. 55, 1984), p.11.

A crucial issue is how to facilitate such Christian communities to empower people to be stewards and sons of God. It is a major contradiction in the Report that, while it talks of people's participation, a major part of its recommendations are to do with the clergy and providing more and better trained clergy. For people's participation we need to talk of enabling the people of God to grow as a community which enables stewardship and identity.

To achieve this more needs to be done than encourage appropriate training for the clergy as the report suggests. We actually need to encourage a change-over from a clergy-dominated leadership which can inhibit participation. We need to examine again biblical models of leadership. In Israelite society in the original settlement the power was decentralized to the elders, the heads of households. These were not the same as the Levites, the temple servants.[1] The New Testament takes over the concept of elders in the household to designate leadership in the institutional church (1 Tim. 5.17). This speaks of a more corporate style of leadership than a one person style usually associated with the parochial ministry. It speaks more of the leadership of heads of households within the church than a description for people with a role as 'temple servants'. If leadership is centred on the clergy alone with a primary focus on what happens in the church building, then at least two things happen. First, the life of a church focuses on itself. But the genius of Anglican missiology at its best is that the life of the church is focused not on itself but on the life of the parish. Second, congregations may be hindered from maturing. Men can specially be marginalized in the life of the church, because they are not given recognition in their role as elders in the wider community, nor space to fulfil a calling as elders in the church fellowship. Since the church provides no space for their fulfilment in this area men often tend to leave involvement in church life to their womenfolk. There seems to have been little teaching in the church in this country on the role of Christian men as stewards, as fathers, as heads of households, or as elders. As a result the teaching of the Christian faith has marginalized the role of men as men. We need to grasp more adequately the biblical themes of stewardship and of the leadership patterns of servanthood and elders. While affirming that neither men nor women can adequately play their roles without a proper relation to each other, and while affirming the insights of biblical feminism, the issue is that men *and* women need liberation in the church today. The teaching which has oppressed women in the church has at the same time oppressed many men. It is teaching which does not take seriously the biblical themes of stewardship and eldership.

Jesus' attacks on the Pharisees in Matthew 23 constantly remind us of the tendency of religious leadership to seek status and lead by domination. In summary we need biblical study and practical models of styles of leadership which truly pastor, empower and enable a community to be a home where people find identity and space to become stewards. The logic of this points to a need of a further report which will tell a theology of story of what Chritian communities, especially among the ethnic minorities in the inner city, are doing, experiencing, and learning. We need this not just to be able to address the inner city but for the whole church to be continually reformed by the good news to the poor.

[1] See C. J. Wright, 'The Ethical Relevance of Israel as a State', in *Transformation* Vol. 1, No. 4, p.11.

3. STRENGTH AND WEAKNESS IN THE CHURCH
by Michael Paget-Wilkes

The Report has been acclaimed as a landmark in the life of the Anglican church for our generation, a prophetic survey that must be acted upon urgently and decisively. And so it is. It has challenged many by its comprehensive survey and assessment of the UPAs of our country, the depth of poverty and disillusionment encountered, and the urgency of the situation for both church and nation. And its unanimous recommendations are being seriously considered by the church as a whole. However, there may be one crucial way in which the Report is both misleading and misguiding us as we seek to respond to the situation described. It comes not so much from the detailed examples and arguments, as from the general impression of the Report which will stay with us long after the details are forgotten. This impression is that, basically speaking, the problem of UPAs can be solved:

(a)   by making more money available from Church and State, and

(b)   by extra assistance being given by the wealthy and powerful.

Clearly, I would fully endorse a redistribution of resources that reduces inequality, alleviates poverty, and narrows the gap between rich and poor, together with the setting up of a Church Urban Fund and the reforms in ministry, method and representation recommended. But the heart of this issue does not lie in what the wealthy can give to the poor or what the central church leadership now wish to grant to UPAs. It does not lie with suburban and village commuter 'success' people giving their 'success' to help others build a similar 'success' story. I deeply believe that *the heart of the issue lies in the fresh and exciting urban spirituality that is emerging from many small local UPA church communities today.* It is this spirituality that needs to be identified, stimulated, and developed; and encouraged to continue to influence and transform life in UPAs. Of course such a spirituality will call for the financing of urban programmes but the *starting point* of action should be 'faith in the city' rather than the Exchequer or Church Commissioners.

It is here that the Archbishop's Commissioners have done the church a sad disservice. They travelled extensively, and heard and received so many reports reflecting the life of many UPA churches, yet they failed adequately to convey in the Report the very real signs of faith, hope, and direction, present in these churches. Maybe they even failed to recognize clearly enough that such faith, hope and activity is both the starting point of new life for those who live in UPAs and also the starting point of transformation for our whole national church and nation. Surely God's words to Paul in 2 Corinthians 12.9 have particular significance and relevance for ourselves in this context—'My grace is all you need, for my power is strongest when you are weak.'

The overall picture of the Report laboriously stresses the weaknesses of UPAs whilst making scant mention of the strengths. Whereas wealth and professional expertise of the rest of the church and nation form the backbone of recommended future action with their weaknesses hardly mentioned. This image leads to the inevitable assumption that UPAs have all the needs and non-UPA churches have all the answers. Such an image must be firmly repudiated before it becomes subconsciously accepted as the right basis for future decisions and actions. Otherwise the Report might just be interpeted as calling for the achievement of suburban living and church standards in UPAs through the injection of money and professional expertise.

Such a conclusion would be disastrous. Suburban living may be seen as the answer in the eyes of the world but certainly not by the biblical standards of a just and God-fearing society. The suburban church may appear to be a more successful model to aim for but actually may well prove to be more of a counterfeit to biblical Christianity than the newly emerging urban spirituality. In the New Testament we read of particular instances where Jesus is profoundly impressed by outstanding faith coming from the most unexpected quarters: such as the faith of the Roman centurion for his servant (Matthew 8.5-13), the woman of Tyre pleading for her daughter's health (Mark 7.24-30), and the woman with a haemorrhage touching Jesus in the crowd (Mark 5.25-35). In my own personal ministry, which includes working in Wandsworth and New Cross, South London, as well as in a town centre church in Rugby, I have found this same extraordinary faith emerging in UPAs where one might least expect to find it. Further evidence of this distinctive faith has been documented by David Driscoll and Greg Smith in their report to ACUPA entitled 'West Ham Church Life Survey 1984'. May I illustrate this kind of faith with some practical examples.

In recent years UPAs have spawned a growing number of churches with a deep understanding of the good news and love of God. This *spirituality* pervades the the life of its members in the face of intense personal pressure and suffering. A resilient faith has emerged despite environmental conditions and distinctly antagonistic attitudes by neighbours and workmates. Vital elements of this faith include 'Proclamation of the gospel and making disciples, Pastoral care of Christians and others, and the Prophetic Christian role of challenging injustice'.[1] This faith leads on to joyous celebration in worship founded on the personal knowledge that God is present and active in their lives. When compared to the spirituality of many suburban churches, not under the same pressures of life, urban spirituality appears particularly impressive and challenging to the outsider or unbeliever. It may not be so eloquently expressed but it can speak straight to the heart.

The overall personal level of *commitment* to the body of Christ is usually far higher in UPA churches and expresses it in different ways. The workload carried and the time given by each member is considerably higher as usually far fewer people have to carry the same basic maintenance, mission and ministry overheads encountered by an church, particularly where UPA churches have more buildings such a Youth and Community Centres, schools, daughter churches etc. Their workload is also swelled by caring for many of the weak and elderly found in UPAs. Need and inadequacy is everywhere, help and support is requested continually, particularly from those whose faith stands firm. Although

[1] See West Ham report, page 54.

12

personal income is comparatively low, UPA churches' giving commitment is often higher per person compared with far wealthier areas. As well as paying high quotas in dioceses with low historic resources, small numbers carry the financial overheads of large and unsuitable buildings. This commitment is also expressed in the depth of personal relationships within the Christian community. There is a strong sense of a corporate family where sorrows and joys, weaknesses and strengths are shared. People matter more than buildings. Obedience to, and participation in, the body is often unconditional, and the quality of fellowship in such churches has increased despite growing difficulties of the last few years.[1]

Living with the deprivations and painfulness of UPAs, as compared with the affluence of the suburbs or the peace of the countryside, often leads to a far deeper sense of *humility* before God. When living with great personal needs one is firstly more aware of human inadequacy to cope which encourages a turning to God for help. When that help comes, his greatness and our weakness is all the more obvious. Also, when surrounded by pleas for personal help and support one is constantly aware of our human inability to cope, and our failure to satisfy all the needy requests. Again, this encourages a turning to the Lord for strength. Such lessons are not so easily identified or learnt in areas where the needs are less acute and where affluence or beauty ease the difficulties of life. Here human ability can cope more adequately and so God's help is not sought except as a last resort. 'Getting on your bike' theology can highlight man's human ability at the expense of humility before God, particularly when one's church is fairly full, financially sound and socially amenable.

When it comes to deciding on church *policy* and *priorities* for ministry and mission UPA churches often make such choices after being forced by circumstances to fundamentally question afresh their biblical roots. Churches in suburban areas quite naturally choose their priorities and policies in the light of a comparative richness of resources e.g. in wealth, numbers and 'knowledge' of the faith. Their churches are bound by strong traditions that are hard to break and can be more culturally rather than biblically orientated. Options chosen could often be described as luxuries rathe than necessities, and they see the Christian life in terms of enjoying the benefits which Christ brings to believers. On the other hand, UPA churches order their priorities in the light of very different circumstances. They have limited human resources, live under pressurized circumstances, including antagonism, scorn and derision from those around them. However, biblical reappraisal has led them to *serve* and *proclaim* their faith to the poor, the weak and oppressed of whom they are a part. They are rediscovering both the justice of God expressed in the Exodus and Old Testament prophets, and also the love of God as expressed in Jesus' total commitment to the outcast, the weak and the unloved in Jewish society.

Finally, many UPA churches could well be described as having a *'corner shop' image* as compared to the more 'supermarket' image of many suburban churches.Church members in UPAs look to the Body of Christ to find a strength of faith to cope with its particular needs. They know personally, and closely identify with, both the 'shop owner' and all the other

[1] See West Ham Report, page 45.

regular customers whom they frequently bump into. Their faith is highly valued and there is a deep sense of belonging to the community. Within the 'Body of Christ' they value warmth and openness, directness and honesty, resilience and communal spirit, humour and family loyalty.[1] Sometimes a suburban church is more reminiscent of a large impersonal supermarket where members only know other people's faces and where the owner is more 'imagined in the mind' than 'real to life'. Church life may well be consumer-orientated, with members going round as private individuals selecting the 'goodies' and going elsewhere if the church does not provide what they want. Or, if the church makes an unpopular decision, members can opt out for a time and rely on their personal faith for a while, returning when matters have returned to normal. People can even chose their church according to the worship style and church life they prefer, often with preference being given to 'entertainment value' (in worship and social function) or 'fringe benefits' (such as good Sunday Schools and creche for the children). Although these descriptions could be seen as a caricature of the reality and although there is also 'consumer-orientation' in UPAs as well, there are still surely lessons to be learnt. If only the embarrassed pain of weakness and failure, normally hidden protectively under the surface of polite yet distant suburban/rural life, could be honestly acknowledged, shared, and tackled together, then surely the depth of personal relationships, and practical appreciation of Christian truths would increase dramatically.

In conclusion therefore, we must go further than seeing the Report as a gigantic 'Band Aid' package from rich to poor. We need to get below the surface of the issue and discover the constantly renewing energy, enthusiasm and strength to be found in some UPA churches which could become a resource for the whole church. (We could even get to the point of admitting that if this quality of urban spirituality were present in suburban and rural church life today then these churches would be making a far greater impact for Christ in their areas than they are at present). We would also need to commit ourselves to stand alongside many others in UPAs who suffer desperately from lack of confidence and selfworth and who live with a continual sense of failure. We could bring to them a fresh vision of God's love for them, his acceptance of them, and his commitment to defeat the evils in society that oppress them so heavily. Such a deeper response to the Report would involve the whole church learning more about UPA life, investing more in the development of UPA church growth, and supporting more the shoots of hope that sprout in society's wastelands. It will mean making money available to develop the churches' ministry in UPAs and working for a more just distribution of resources in society. But most of all, when all the publicity and debate have died down, let us become committed to change the life of our church so that the joy of the resurrection rises out of the pain, suffering and weakness of UPA areas, and so that the faith of the Roman centurion becomes the faith of the whole church. Let us see how this faith is in line with many churches in third world countries where the faith of the weak is growing at an extraordinary rate compared with the so-called established wealthy churches of the West. And, let us do it because it is a true reflection of the life, death and resurrection of Jesus Christ, who is the head of his Body—our Church.

[1] See West Ham Report, page 50.

14

4. ECONOMIC COST AND HUMAN HOPE
by Roy McLoughry

The message of the *Faith in the City* Report is very clear. Poverty expressed as powerlessness, inequality or polarization, exists not because of the indifference of society but because, in the words of the Report,

> 'The UPA is of our own making. The combination of our private pre-ferences and the ramifications of our political choices are returned to us here as the geographical dimension of an unequal society.' (para.1.50, p.25)

It is because the system which produces such poverty is *not* neutral that Christians are called to exercise moral judgment in economics and politics and where they are found wanting, to call for reform in the name of justice. Yet the quote above shows us that we cannot vent our anger on politicians and decision-makers if the system which they represent reflects our own secret preferences. Many people *prefer* the poor to be housed in UPA tower blocks because such isolation provides a simple means of not having to deal with their 'problems' (let alone get involved with their lives or offer friendship!). Such a polarization is a part of the social order, a means of control. It is no wonder that private charity cannot cope with such a complex social problem for, as Berdayev once said, 'a person's fate cannot be made to rest solely upon other people's spiritual condition.'[1] It is one thing to give to Liveaid for 'them' in the Third World; it would be quite another to attempt it for 'us' in the urban jungles of modern Britain.

The Economic Point of View
The Commission concludes its Report by saying, 'we present no com-prehensive political or economic analysis. That task goes beyond this commission' (15.8 p.360). It is well known that, with two exceptions[2], the Commission did not attempt to cost its recommendations, partly because it was presenting a vision to be heeded rather than a programme to be costed but also because it saw this role as the responsibility of those who wielded more power than the Commission and who had more expertise to hand. Despie these good intentions, the Report is sufficient-ly infused with the economic point of view for the absence of figures to be a cause for concern. The Commission's own defence would doubtless be that they were trying to outline not a programme, but rather agenda; a recording of priorities that would start a debate, rather than a detailed programme which by definition assumes that the debate has reached definite conclusions.

Nevertheless, it is here that a conflict shows itself within the Report between moral authority and economic precision. We are currently living in a political vacuum in which the traditional left-right divide is sterile and the centre coalition often seems to represent pragmatism in search of

---

[1] *The Destiny of Man* (1937), p.120.
[2] The exceptions being the extension of the Community Programme (para. 9.80) and the extension of the long-term rate of supplementary benefit to those umemployed for more than one year (para. 9.90).

success. It is not obvious who will provide a new moral vision to motivate and energize our lack-lustre performance. It does not seem that it will come from the traditional political parties. Does the *Faith in the City* Report represent a strong claim by the Church to have the right to speak out on these issues?

There is a considerable gulf between 'Blessed are you who hunger now, for you will be satisfied' (Luke 6.21) and a political programme to feed the hungry, or between 'Blessed are the peacemakers' and government policy on Cruise missiles. As one moves down the ladder of abstraction from the moral vision to the practical programme, the Christian content diminishes. At the point of implementation of a White Paper there is no Christian content in it at all. It is only when the Christian M.P. is asked about the rationale behind his bill that he points to its Christian roots (as the Marxist would point to his). In a pluralistic democracy there are many ways of implementing the same vision and some means may have their roots equally firmly in a Christian moral vision. It is difficult to commit oneself to outlining the Christian foundations of a complex and controversial subject and then go all the way in outlining a specific set of programmes knowing that alternatives exist which are equally feasible. The understandable half-way house is to stop at the 'agenda' rather than the 'programme'. The cost of doing this is that those opposed to the recommendations can put their own cost on the outcome, others find it easier to ignore the recommendations because they are 'woolly' still others can claim that it is easy to produce fine-sounding sentiments when one does not have to show where the money is coming from.

Viewing life through the eyes of 'the economic point of view' forces one to play the game according to its rules. The report is not self consciously critical enough about the nature of the tools it uses, otherwise it might have avoided some of the problems outlined above by pointing out that the use of economic categories largely rules out moral debate. Economic efficiency has come to dominate moral categories in the years since the enlightenment and those who wish to recover a moral authority in the field of economics will find themselves in difficulties until they use its tools with extreme caution.

Structures and Individuals
Two messages come across in the report, one is the intransigence of the problems in the UPAs and their structural nature; the other is the message . . . 'we have found faith in the city.' The first statement brings a dark foreboding about the future of those living in UPAs the latter brings a message of hope, showing that the human spirit is capable of generating hope in the midst of bleakness and that powerlessness does not mean hopelessness.

Early in the section of the Report which addresses the church the importance of an incarnational theology is stressed. But should those who see their ministry in terms of coming alongside to help others in their struggle be comfortable with the language of structures with which to describe their problems? Of course the urban pastor is drawn daily into the problems of structural evil and obduracy, as his pastoral concern leads him into conflict with injustice in council housing policy, racial discrimination in the mortgage market and the usual all-too-familiar tensions between his parishioners and the police. Here, however, it is the use of the *language* of structures which provides difficulties, for as a means of describing a problem it can add to its intransigence and seemingly rule out the second message of the Report—that there is hope in the city because of the people of the city.

Many people who are convinced that the problems of the inner city are deeply structural and intransigent, because of the unjust behaviour of the major institutions of our society, are faced with a difficult choice. If they choose to work through those institutions to bring about change then they extend legitimacy to them. If they reject this option then they themselves are forced onto the margins of the debate with propaganda and protest as their only weapons, which are easily disregarded. Yet this problem can be an artificial consequence of the way in which the prolems are expressed.

In adopting the language of 'structures' one stresses the interdependence of local, national, and international, pressures on modern urban life. Much that happens to a particular city occurs because of international economic phenomena rather than because of the problems within the city itself, particularly if the wealth of the city is dependent on a few 'sunset' industries which are 'sunrise' industries elsewhere in the world. The use of 'freezing the action' and providing a 'snapshot' of all these interrelated pressures should be obvious. The enormity of the problem is often successful in persuading governments that only national or intenational initiatives can succeed. Repair jobs are out.

The language of structures provides a static picture, its success depends on taking events and relationships which are always changing and evolving and presenting them simultaneously to enable them to be analysed and compared. Such a picture is both comprehensive and compelling but these very qualities make change harder to conceive of. As relationships are drawn into the image they become almost predetermined and resistant to change. As one commentator has said, 'change can only come from outside, but if a structural metaphor is applied to society as a whole, who is the external agent?'[1]

Such a metaphor takes social conformity as a given, as if people's behaviour is determined by the socio-economic pressures on them. But people do not behave as if they were conforming socially. They act according to their own perception of the world around them and do not perceive the choices before them, however limited, as the invitable outcome of the situation they are in. When the Commission engaged in analysis, they came to a conclusion that the problems which were facing the inner cities were seemingly intractable: when they stayed with the people who were facing the problems they found faith and hope as well as anger:

> 'We know that there is a transforming power present in human affairs which can resolve apparently intractable situations and bring new life into the darkest places.' (15.9 p.360)

[1] Peter Marris *Community Planning and Concepts of Change* (RKP, 1982) pp.110-129 are especially relevant.

Trade unionism, the women's movement and the civil rights movement began when individuals decided that they did not need to conform to the pattern of behaviour expected of them because they were unjust. A few people showed others that it was possible to swim against the tide and a movement was born as a result, albeit at great human cost. Although at present we recognize the powerlessness of those who live in UPAs they are not helped by language which emphasizes their powerlessness but need the encouragement to see the permanent change can come through the strength of the human spirit rather than through government programmes (though these are extremely important).

One of the criticisms of the Report as a whole is that its recommendations are too heavily dependent on the actions of a centralized government initative. The reason for this may lie partly in the fact that the emphasis of the Report was more on the structural economic and social forces which have created the problems rather than the kind of partnerships between industry, local authority, and the voluntary sector, which may provide the seeds of hope for the future. More examples of these signs of hope would have been most welcome (as has been alluded to elsewhere in this booklet).

Problems and Solutions
If the first tension in the Report is between its moral vision and its economic 'agenda' and the second between the use of impersonal structural pictures and human stories of hope the third tension is between the language of problems and solutions and the persistence of failure in the UPAs. This third tension is closely allied to other two. The *Faith in the City* Report, being an official report on the plight of the UPAs, had of course to use the language of analysis and commentary very effectively in order to be read and heeded by those in power, and this it did. But the problem with the language of analysis is that it necessarily abstracts from the lives of ordinary people which are more accurately conveyed in narrative and story. The lives of people in the UPAs can be seen as a vast jigsaw puzzle, the picture of which is determined by the 'snapshot' we talked about in the previous section on structures. A problem is seen as a missing bit of the jigsaw and various solutions are tried until one fits.

But life is rarely perceived in this way by those living in the UPAs. If they are wary of the Report it is because promises and recommendations have been made about their lives for the last fifty years. Their memories are long and their expectations (to their mind) are realistic. When they say that the problems of housing, unemployment, and poverty, will still be present in fifty years time, who is there to contradict them? If, as we mooted at the outset of this section, the existence of the UPAs reflects our darkest hidden preferences, then our attempts to change the situation will be thwarted. Yet Christians are notoriously bad at coping with what they see as failure. We have identified the 'blessing of God' with the success of our programme of action. Other sections of theis Report point out that the vitality and spiritual life found in the midst of the difficulties of the UPA show that what from one viewpoint may be regarded as deprivation, powerlessness, inadequacy and structural evil may from another

18

viewpoint be the fertile soil in which the words 'blessed are you who are poor for yours is the kingdom of God' (Luke 6.20) become a living reality in a way in which they never could be in a suburban setting.

From the standpoint of the Christian economist these three tensions are as important as the details of the report's economics. They affect the permanent impact which it will have both on the Church and on the nation. The tension between moral authority and economic 'agenda', between structural analysis and individual story and derived from this, the tension between the analysis of 'problems and solutions' and the story of human hope in the face of adversity are important to grapple with. it is a credit to the report that it manages to cope with these tensions, to inform us strategically and yet warm our hearts, to the challenge both church and nation and yet also inspire the individual to greater commitment to those who live in the UPAs. Above all, in pointing to the creation of the UPAs as a reflection of our own preferences it lays upon us a collective obligation from which we attempt to escape only at a high cost for the future of our society. For this painful insight alone we should be truly grateful.

5. LIFE IN THE CITY
by Greg Forster

The Archbishop's Commission affirm on many occasions in their Report that they have seen examples of faith at work in the city, and that this gives them grounds for great hope and confidence. No doubt they felt that lack of space prevented them from actually giving details of most of the examples which they saw. As a result the Report was perhaps vulnerable to being dismissed as merely another official report—an Orange-and-Blue Paper—whereas part of the Christian contribution to any debate on the inner cities and estates and their problems is that we sit where they sit; we can speak because we are there among those who live with the problem, and we find God is there too. Perhaps he does not 'solve' the problem, but he is 'not unable to sympathize with our weakness'.

In this chapter we attempt to describe a few examples of what gives rise to hope in the city. They are limited by space, and the access we have to suitable examples to describe. We do not claim that they are perfect examples of good practice, or that they are total 'success stories', but we do believe that they are ways in which God is at work. Nor do we claim theological or even political 'soundness' for all that is done, but perhaps mission has untidy edges; it was made for man, not man for mission.

The areas of Moss Side and Longsight in Manchester became by-words in 1981 with the inner city troubles then. Many community groups work in that area, some established by the local authority, others by churches, others based on localities or political interests.

The Longsight Moss Side Community Project is one such. The initiative to establish it came from several local churches. It works in several fields; two workers are involved in community education, one building up informal groups where Asian women can learn both language and skills appropriate for life in Britain, and finding that a great deal of case-work and counselling of individuals comes her way; the other seeks to support or establish groups which can work for their own needs in the community—holiday clubs for children, neighbourhood groups trying to improve the state of houses, traffic flow, policing, etc., in their particular group of streets. Recently one of these workers commented to me that though no policy existed of looking for leaders for such groups among the churches, a significantly high proportion of those who took leadership roles in the groups were active church members—either their faith, or their experience of leadership within the church, or the confidence that it gave them, enabled them to contribute to the general wellbeing of their area.

The project employs two other workers researching into the employment needs of the area, and then establishing small workshops to meet those needs. Garment manufacturing has proved the most suitable trade to work with, in line with both the potential skills of the population, and the demand for skills from commercial concerns in the area. Funding has been obtained from MSC and from the City Council to run two workshops. One began as a training workshop, the other under the Community Programme offers (officially) no training but repairs garments, etc., for the use of or sale by charitable organisations. It remains MSC funded, and employs 24 people. The other workshop has gone independent, despite the problems of losing MSC funding, and makes up garments on contract for commercial wholesalers.

It was originally hoped that it would become a cooperative, but the legal commitments of this proved too daunting for the trainee/workers involved. However, as a workshop of employees it illustrates how local initiative, backed by carefully targetted government and local authority grants, can contribute to a local economy. For a local authority outlay of about £3000 p.a. on premises, and an Urban Programme grant of under £10,000 for the supporting community worker, relatively permanent employment is provided for four to six workers, saving their 'dole' payment, and bringing their contribution into the ecomony. But it is not just economic value which is gained from this exercise. If the same workers worked from home they would lack the respect gained from a definite job, and the security to fall back on derived from National Insurance payments. Nor are they as vulnerable to the pressures of the work-supplier as they would be as lone home workers.

The project originally was the brain child of one of the local clergy, Gerry Wheale, who also lectures in Community Development at Manchester University. It is this approach to community self-help which provides the philosophy behind the project. For instance, if it appears from the field work done by one of the workers that a youth club is desirable in a certain area, the project does not set it up itself, but provides the knowhow and contacts for people in the area to do so for themselves; it helps them to fulfil legal requirements which enable them to qualify for grants, and gives the encouragement to carry on through the difficulties and disagreements found by people perhaps unused to 'committee' work. In doing so it lets them discover how to run their own thing.

Translating that into theological terms, it enables people to discover their own worth, and exercise their own gifts, as they take their own part in the outworking of God's Common Grace to mankind. On this level at least a team made up of Muslims, a Hindu and Christians can work together for the upbuilding of the various communities in the area.

In the light of the recommendations of the Archbishop's Commission, it is perhaps worth noting that grants for the support of the main project come from the Government's Urban Programme via the Local Authority (c. 75%) and from the Mothers' Union and Manchester Diocese (c 25%). If this kind of centrally funded support for local projects is what the Commission had in mind when it called for more Government and church funds for the inner cities and estates, then we have no quarrel with them. But we (the authors of this booklet) believe that it must be this kind of scheme, in which local people are enabled to find power over their own lives, and not some scheme which is handed down from above, and whose administration is in the hands of church or state officials. We in LMSCP find the requirements of MSC accounting and grant renewal applications, which are far more exacting than normal commercial procedures, both onerous and condescending (even while we accept our responsibility to give good account of our stewardship of public money).

A further example of Church action for the benefit of a community in the inner city is the Churches' Work Scheme. This also functions in inner

Manchester, and is sponsored by the Hulme and Moss Side Christian Fellowship. It has been working for about eighteen months (as at March 1986) and is funded by MSC's Community Programme. As of writing 66 people are employed in a number of different tasks. Of these twenty-four are full-time, including the supervisors; the rest are part-timers. Some are relandscaping the grounds of one of the churches in the locality. Others are renovating furniture which they acquire through house clearances, gifts, etc., and it is then made available to charitable organizations or individuals who are in need, as vouched for by local social services, churches, etc. Where possible they are asked to make a donation towards the cost of these items, though it does not amount to a commercial rate for the work done or cost of the materials used. The project may not make a profit—nor can any CP scheme according to the rules, which means that it is very hard for such schemes to cease being dependent on handouts, even when they would like very much to go independent. However, it is expected to show a surplus of £3000 in a year, which is 'clawed back' from the grant which it receives.

As well as landscaping work, and furniture refurbishment the project hopes to begin another field of work soon, restoring old tools. They also hope that their resources in keeping accounts will become available to former workers on the scheme, and others in the area who might wish to start up their own small businesses, but who lack the bookkeeping skills which are necessary for the running of a business, even when they have the technical skill such as cabinet making or french polishing. Once again the hope of the management committee of the scheme is that those involved will acquire not only work experience and a skill, but also a sense of self worth and confidence through doing a job, and doing it well over a period, (though as with the CP work done by LMSCP it is not officially permitted to offer training under this scheme—only work which will benefit the 'community' may be done. Somehow in the official mind the community can be divorced from the individuals who make it up, so that it is no benefit to the community for its members to gain economic security and independence from the handouts of the state!).

Pastor Ronnie Blake and Fr. Phil Sumner, who described the work of the scheme to me, spoke of their desire to help all those whom society has rejected, not just church members, and to build up their confidence. I was told of one lad who had worked successfully with the project for some time. Someone who knew him said to Pastor Blake, 'I didn't know he would ever go into work.' That is one individual's success story, but it is also a sign of hope for the whole of that community, for the atmosphere is created in which people can say, 'If he can do it, so can I, and so can my children.' Out of such small successes is built Hope for the City.

But not every story has a happy ending. I was also introduced to a lad who had worked successfully on the scheme for the permitted twelve months, and then, with good references, had got a job with a chain of retail newsagents in the Manchester area. He had worked well with them, but it involved acting as a stand-in when people were off at other branches. This meant that he, a black, had to serve at the counters in newsagents in some of the more 'select' neighbourhoods in the county. It appears that he was subjected to till checks and other difficulties by the management, and finally was dismissed simply as being not suitable. I suppose it cannot be proved that he was dismissed because his colour was unacceptable in the 'select' suburbs, but that was the impression that he had, and that his former employers in the scheme also had. Those who do not have faith in those of the city can do a great deal, almost unconsciously, (or am I being too charitable to them?) to undermine the hope that there is there.[1]

While it is important that the search to create new jobs goes on, and that the church be involved in this as best it can, there is also need to be realistic. The economic trends are such that large-scale long-term unemployment is sure to be with us for some years yet. What people need to discover is that life can have purpose and direction without paid employment. This is the basic philosophy underlying the Impasse centres which have mushroomed in the Cleveland area in recent years. Impasse had its roots in an initiative launched by Bill Hall, the Arts and Recreation Chaplain in the North East, in the late 1960s. Its aim is to provide the resources for unemployed people to be as creative as possible, to develop new and existing skills and interests. The largest Impasse centre at Middlesbrough contains a woodwork shop, craft rooms for silk-screening, tapestry, weaving, photography, etc., a garage where vehicles can be serviced and rebuilt, a tool library with a membership over 1000, a restaurant which specializes in cooking on a tight budget, and much else besides. The Impasse Volunteer line encourages unemployed people to do gardening, decorating and other jobs for the elderly, disabled and other disadvantaged people in the community. Through Impasse many have discovered that life without a paid job need not be boring and demoralizing.

These centres have been built up gradually over the last 15 years, and have depended a lot on the Manpower Services Commission for funding. But the initiative came from local people, notably a clergyman with a particular concern for the unemployed, not from the state. Although Impasse is unusual in the scale on which it operates, church-backed resource centres for the unemployed are increasing in number. They can be misconstrued or poorly presented as seeking to sugar the pill of unemployment. When developed in an imaginative way which flows out of the needs and desires of local unemployed people, however, they open up exciting possibilities of a whole new way of thinking about life, work and the connection between the two.

[1] In this connection an observation from the 'West Ham Church Life Survey 1984' (a report to the Archbishop's Commission on Urban Priority Areas, prepared by Rev. David Driscoll and Greg Smith) September 1984, page 49 is apposite,
'At the personal level problems were seem to lie most of all at the level of powerlessness, apathy and lack of self confidence. Repeatedly respondents from all sections of church life were stressing that local people had no self confidence, a low self image, a lack of self respect or pride, but always without blaming the people themselves. Rather as one respondent put it, it is the negative images and stereotypes of the area conveyed by the media, and (we would add) by schools and the church that has robbed people of their sense of self worth. In this context the gospel message which many churches are rediscovering is that in God's eyes every individual is immensely valuable and that in Christ the fullness of human dignity can be restored.

Is all this properly part of the churches' mission? Phil Sumner, as chairman of his project, reckons on visiting it each day, encouraging and showing interest, and he finds that the pastoral opportunities this gives him with employees are many, quite apart from the contribution all this gives to the morale of the community, and to its economic viability.

My own commitment to LMSCP is not so heavy, but if I describe my impressions of a visit today it will testify to the faith that there is in the city; perhaps, as Michael Paget-Wilkes suggests in his section, a more vital faith than that of the suburbs. We were visited by a Government minister touring the area in connection with a new scheme to support inner cities. Some of our girls took him on in debate, with courtesy but firmness, arguing that more trust should be placed in people from the inner cities in running the new scheme; that there was a great deal of skill and ability there, but perhaps a difficulty in creating the capital or obtaining it to set up local businesses. After he left they were talking about their success or otherwise in making their point. The closing remark of one of them was worthy of a Nehemiah; that we had made our points as clearly as we could, and now should pray to God that the minister remembered them and was prepared to act on them. Earlier another of the workers had taken me to one side to talk about his faith, to ask about mine, and to share a message—perhaps I should say prophecy—with me. There is great faith to learn from in the City.

In Conclusion
Richard Higginson comments that on reading or learning about the Report many people will have wondered how it would affect them or their church. For many who live outside the inner cities, or the city-edge estates, the mass of statistics produced in *Faith in the City* is such a mass as to be overwhelming. It seems too daunting to take in, let alone act upon. Faced with such enormity it is a very natural reaction for the finite individual who is not in the midst of the situation to say, 'It can't really be as bad as that,' or to do nothing and hope that 'they' will sort it out. Another reaction is to develop a sense of guilt because we are unable to do enough to 'solve' the problem, and this in turn also leads to a feeling of paralysis.

Recently, because of the massive ecological disasters in East Africa, people's reaction to information about disasters and problems has been studied in detail. One of the points which has arisen from this study is that we naturally react to people, in relationship, rather than to blocks of information. Where a relationship exists, or can be generated, then action is more manageable. Where the 'problem' is a set of figures without a human face it is intractable, or even unimaginable.

The small-scale developmental approach which we have advocated in this collection of essays does offer a manageable response to people's need—perhaps just as Jesus met the needs of the 5,000 with the question to one individual, 'What have you got?', and then took it on from there. It is possible to relate to one community scheme here, or one counselling group there, and within the Christian church the theological relationship exists between the 'body of all faithful people', which can be developed on a practical level. The companion booklet in the Pastoral Series[1] looks at this in greater detail, but it is a two-way relationship in which secular social status is not automatically spiritual riches.

[1] David Newman (ed.) *On from Faith in the City* (Grove Pastoral Series no. 26, 1986).